Lulzim Tafa
TERRIBLE SONGS

Albanian poetry from Kosovo

Lulzim Tafa

TERRIBLE SONGS

English version by **Patricia Lidia**
Foreword by **Peter Tase**

GRACIOUS LIGHT
NEW YORK

2013

Copyright@Lulzim Tafa, 2013

Original title: *Cântece teribile*
English version by: Patricia Lidia

SERIES: Albanian Literature

Series Editor: Baki Ymeri
Editorial advisor: Theodor Damian, Eduard M. Dilo,
Laura Rushani
Cover: Alban Voka

This book appears in collaboration with the Albanian
Cultural Union from Romania and
The Association of Albano-American Writers

Published by Gracious Light Publishing House
New York 2013
30-18 50th Street, Woodside, NY 11377, USA

ISBN: 978-1-888067-37-8

SHORT BIO-BIBLIOGRAPHY

Lulzim Tafa was born near Prishtina, the capital of Kosovo, on 1970. He is one of the renowned poets of the turbulent times of 1990 in Kosovo, a country that was constantly experiencing ethnic cleansing and mass killings of its people by the Serbian war machine. After his elementary and high school education in his native village of Lipian, Tafa attended the School of Law in the University of Prishtina and became an attorney four years later, in early 1992. Mr. Tafa pursued graduate studies in the University of Sarajevo and received his Ph.D. degree in Law.

Apart from his scholarly works in the field of law and social sciences, Lulzim Tafa, has written many volumes in Albanian Literature. Until now he has published a number of poetry books: *Blood Won't Become Water* (Rilindja Press, Prishtina, 1993), *Sadness Metaphor* (Rilindja Press, Prishtina, 1997), *Planet of Babylon,* Stage poetry (Rilindja Press, Prishtina, 1999), *I Still Have Two Words* (Faik Konica Press, Prishtina, 2011) *Work for the Devil,* Selected poetry (Gjordan-Studio, Sarajevo, 2011), *Dream Exhibition* (Amanda Edit, Bucharest, 2012).

Tafa's literary works have been translated into several languages, he is the recipient of several literary awards and is included in many anthologies of poetry. Lulzim Tafa is active in many Human Rights projects. He writes poems, prose and conducts studies in literary criticism and journalism. He is full professor in several universities in Kosovo and abroad. Currently is serving as Rector of the AAB University in Prishtina.

FOREWORD

The Republic of Kosova is the youngest independent nation of Europe, but surprisingly it is one of the ancient cradles equipped with a wealth of poetry and literature in the Old Continent. Kosova's lasting legacy in poetry, literary critism and prose is represented with a high level of professionalism in all books of poetry that are written in the last two decades by Lulzim Tafa, begining with his first poetry book, *Blood Won't Become Water* and continued by many other literary projects that have helped the author master the use of words, metaphor, style as well as allegory. Tafa's artistic use of all these meticulous elements have made him a unique voice of poetry in Europe and beyond.

A few days before the publication of *Terrible Songs* I had the privilege to read and appreciate Mr. Tafa's verses and observe closely his passion about poetry, the encompassing of nature in most of his verses and above all the first hand experience of the suffering and longing that the author himself had endured in a time of violent conflict in Kosovo that lasted many years and reached a fragile peace only after the NATO intervention of 1998-1999. Lulzim Tafa's verses are an expression of and influenced by the tumultuous environment – a region engulfed in decades long ethnic cleansing campaigns conducted by Serbian forces - created in the Balkans in the 1990, even though occasionally the author has intertwined his sentimental feelings in many sad verses and refers to the Sun as a source of punishment, hope and salvation. In verses of *You Slept Under the Moon* and *Ancient City* Tafa uses the presence of the Sun in an admirable and punishable context: "Don't you pity me?/ Let the sun hurt your eyes?/ You slept under the shadow of the moon/ And I stayed nil while hiding you in the song/ Why are you crying?" and "Blows a slight icy breeze/ The ancient city of the wind oscillates his eyelids/ I am no fool to want you/ Ancient city of first love."

In these verses the reader is able to deduce Tafa's figurative language that includes in a single canvas a myriad of colors, expressions, aspirations and longing. All these details have typical colors that are represented through orbital objects, such as the Sun, the Moon, and inner world fantasy of dreams, oscillations of eye lids and feelings of love. A few minutes after reading Tafa's verses, they made me think of Edgar Allan Poe who considered "poetry as the rhythmical creation of beauty in words," this is perhaps exactly what every reader will experience while reading Tafa's poetry.

As I was reaching the last poems of his volume, Tafa's structure of verses, rhyme, context and pathos continued to rise, even though the topic had slightly changed and was focused more on the war of Kosova and the tragic loss of human life. In *Death Predict* Lulzim Tafa describes the chaotic conditions during the Kosovo War of Independence: "I will be killed in this war/ For each button/ Of the

7

jacket/ I'll take a bullet/ And every drop of blood/ Button will become/ In the shirts and jackets/ Of my/ Soldiers and captains...". The poem starts with a tragic prediction, which unfortunately is in the minds of every citizen who hears night and day the frightening rifle shots in the nearby hills covered by trenches and well trained KLA soldiers fighting well trained Serbian forces. Another component illustrated in Tafa's verses is the overall war environment in Kosovo's cities.

It is heartbreaking, although the situation is vividly described, how Lulzim Tafa's fellow countrymen were affected by war, famine, destruction and how almost all of them were turned into landless refugees, empty handed human beings carrying only their mere clothes. The tragic consequences of War, are deeply rooted in Tafa's verses and as a result they make all of us sympathize with him and many other war refugees who are brokenheartedly connected to the following verses in *War Atmosphere* and *The Patriots:* "In Kosova those days/ Became more expensive/ Bread/ Oil/ Corn/ Only life's/ Price/ Had fallen/ We had in abundance/ Death." and "I love more/ The country,/ He kisses its land then,/ He curses himself on stones and slabs..."

Through these verses Lulzim Tafa has introduced the global reader with a world region that has produced a history of barbaric conflicts, bloodshed and innocent victims. It is certain that Tafa's soul is with his countrymen. He acknowledges the endless pain of violence and is hopeful for a better future for his homeland.

Tafa's native soil is depicted in his poetry through intense emotions that turn into spoken and articulated thoughts, which later turn into radiant words. According to Plato "Poetry is nearer to vital truth than history." This great philosopher has given us the best definition of a genuine poetry that resembles Tafa's writing style, substance and coherence.

Peter Tase

Dream Exhibition

SUNDAYS DO NOT CALL ME

Sundays do not call me
Maybe I won't wake up
Forever remaining in the sleep of death.
Do not forget the frozen moments
Only on Sundays your day is chosen.
For you, when I die
After seven mountains,
I will seek your name.
Ah! why don't you come on other days

TEUTA

Tonight I call you Teuta
To go to the pub Poison
That your tongue draws out.
Your eyes - harbingers of ice
In the broken branch
Of the silent destiny.
Teuta
Gods bow before you.

I REMEMBER YOUR FACE

I remember your face
The blood - frozen tear
Covering me.

I remember your language
A snake - black poison
Wrapping my destiny.

When you sleep
I wake up
With your memory.

RESIGNATION

If you want
You take the comb and
Hairdressing the Night
As a flapper...

Dye her nails...

PATHETIC DECLARATION

So that I die for you
You are so good Fairy
How heavy are
Those wires...

THE MOON

At least your work
If I knew
After a lunatic communication
Nightly
The moon
Clear or gloomy.

YOU SLEPT UNDER THE MOON

Don't you pity me?
Lest the sun hurt your eyes?
You slept under the shadow of the moon
And nilly i hid you in the song.
Why are you crying?
Aren't you sorry that the eyes
Will come in your song
And I'll forget the way back?
From the mischievous wailing,
From the black dream,
Please don't cry
Don't you pity me, child?

ANCIENT CITY

A slight breeze blows icy
The ancient city the wind shakes his eyelids.

I am no fool to want you
Ancient city of first love.

With hands roads to measure
Ancient city without stone castle

That works like the clock.

HERMETIC

I'll close you
It will hurt to open you up
Not even you know where you are
Not even the sea will not be seen
Not even the dust
Will no longer
Do
Zap...

WILL RAIN TOMORROW

We won't see each other tomorrow
it's Sunday
And it will rain

We will sleep a century.

I don't know
The sun will come
Or we will see each other
After the sunny rain.

It will be raining tomorrow
I will bow to you
To your eyes
To the wretched Gods.

I do not know if the Lord is crying
or it rains
We will not see each other tomorrow
When it will rain.

Tomorrow we will die together.

YOU BROUGHT THE TIMES
TO SLEEP UNDER THE MOON

Only the nails remained nails
Tomorrow brings something new
With the old yesterday we bled.
The horse in the rain
How many drops bit you that day
When other shoppers came too
Grapes and pumpkins sellers
To change destinies.
He looked up to the sky
The sun does not intend to set
Today either
The rain will stop someday
One day yes one day.
It is said that the rain does not melt the horse
The horse lying in the rain and dries
in the breeze
The innumerable
unbridled
godless horse
the horse steamed in the rain.

TOMORROW

We will sit again Teuta
On wooden chairs
Toast vitreous glasses
As fate as hearts.
Again to sit
Memories to live
To read the verses
Of written nights.
Give me eyes to see the sun
How stars fall
As the sky falls.
We will sit again, Teuta
To tell the dreams
Of written nights.
With eyes open the dawn to catch
Again we will sit
On wooden chairs
Be careful Teuta
Of life
Of death
Be careful...

GOOD RAINY NIGHT

Good rainy night
the silence of the city kills
the late seasons
the late traveler
in the wet city.

Light rainy night
the late traveler
in the wet city
puts tonight
a mortuary
crown

Light night with rain
do not destroy my traces
in the city smelling of blood.

IN OUR ABSENCE

We are not anymore
One of us died
The other was killed by the army
Some in exile
We grieved so much
After a day.

The girlfriends of our class
Some wait for the black trains
Some have become women of exiled men
And went with lamentations.

Only one stopped
At the class door has shortened the hair
Giving signs that we
Will forget each other.

THE POETS

When gods get angry
Poets are born.
At the first sign of life
They rise against their masters.
They protest
When they grow
Become wink
Spread posters
Against themselves
As demonstrators in the city
"The additional child of any mother
Becomes a poet "...

WHEN I WILL DIE

When I will die
Do not cry baby
I betrayed you
With the virgins of another planet.

When I will die do not cry sister
I gallop on Gherghi's horse *
Over the waves of the sea...

When I will die do not cry mother
Only nurse
these
melancholic
metaphors
as you nursed me once...

_____

* Gjergj Elez Alia, a folk character

DREAMS EXPLANATORY THEORY

If you have seen in your dream the Snake
Someone stopped your game.

If you have seen in your dream the Freedom
Someone flirts with your Slavery.

If you have seen in your dream my eyes
Someone cheated you.

I told you stubborn
I told you
Do not sleep
Because dreams take out
The love through your nose...

PATHS

(A)

They have no beginning and no end
There are headless paths
They are paths
That intersect themselves
There are paths with no path
But the path
Is always
Found
You start
Come
Good journey...

COMPLEX

Two prostitutes
Beautiful
Goddesses
Drink coffee and follow
In the cup
The lines and the paths.
They paint their toenails
As usually
Arouse desires
And dreams at sea
Birds in the sky
In this world...

(Istanbul, 2001)

CHILLS

The pain map
Tattooed on the lips
Can read
The way you go.

The hard
and cold chills
of fever's
lively chills...

Look where they appeared
But you have no fault
That you can't read
This absurd art
Of lines on the lips...

Terrible Songs

DEATH PREDICTS

I will be killed in this war
For each button
Of the jacket
I'll take a bullet
And every drop of blood
Button will become
In the shirts and jackets
Of my
Soldiers and captains...

TERRIBLE SONGS

Oh sir the evils
Rise and come
We expect the in our chest
Humble, we bow our head.
Oh sir the evils
Come before dawn
Chain of bullets
And girdle with cutters
Oh sir
And angry become without fear
Over the prudent necks
Over the calm chest.
Oh sir
And rise and come
Watch over us God...

Here they come ...

(Prishtina, 1999)

THE POWERFUL

I.

The powerful
Attack Kosovo
With modern armored cars
With bulletproof
Clothes
And hoods.

With national
And heavenly
Support
The massacre was legitimate
Backed up by paragraph 1
About killing all Albanians...

II.

They were the most human murderers
Glorious
Killed indiscriminately
Men
Women
Children...

They were killing and singing
My God
God helped them...

Your God
To be killed
By my Lord ...

(1998)

THE FIGHTERS

Last night
I could not sleep
I do not know if we have bread
For tonight
And gunpowder
For tomorrow...

(1999)

WAR ATMOSPHERE

In Kosovo, those days,
Became more expensive
Bread
Oil
Corn
Only life's
Price
Had fallen
We had in abundance
Death.

POPPY THIEVES

Not because blood was shed
Not because infants
Had shrapnel sown in their cheeks.

But because blood
Was shed
And the man
Like a poppy
Was torn...

BAPTISMS

Do not baptize children
With the names Mërgim*
Urtak**
Durim***
Because our mountains remain
Without heroes...

———————
* *Exile*
** *Prudent*
*** *Patience*

REASON

The first child
Who was born this summer
Was baptized Durim
And every day
My imaginary fruits
Dry.

Thank God grandpa
is not alive.

I go as the old people say
With the unquenchable desire
Of the red apple...

WE

All we did was
To get dressed
And undressed
Of metaphors.

We dressed up
And undressed
The skin
Of oaks...

With the shroud
We germinated
The offspring.

We forgot the homeland
Of the shroud
Of love...

And of beautiful...

REPORT OF THE HOLY FIGHT

We the servants of the fight run upward
We do not know whereto we started
Or where we reach for to the light
They are watching us surrounded us
With their boots and iron teeth of fight
We barefoot unshaven hungry
Unwashed for a week with hair like wire
Threads- threads the soul
we chew the despair
We spit the pieces of the bloody destiny
And the lively words got stuck to our tongues
They talk we are silent and fall in circles
Raise our hands surrender to the wolf
Fall at its mercy
At its teeth and trorn eye
Our eyes grow
Three rapists swept over a woman
What unequal battle of destiny
In front of our porn eyes alive she appears
Minor children can also see her
That stay in cold's tail
Our sex's wrection does not wake us
We are covered by the death's erection
Poor you good woman
Lively flesh have we waken up
The fight emigrated to other life
And only the mountain mighties with wings

FREE TERRITORIES

The territories were free
And we were also
The day was long and happy
We kissed under an apple tree
Suddenly rockets began to fall
The free territories
Have changed to deserted territories
Deserted we became too
I wonder
Who kisses now there
Under that deserted apple tree...

THREE DAYS ALBANIA

Oh Lord let...
And if we become ashes
We were happy
In those three days of Albania...

REPORT OF KOSOVA '99

Here the human rights and freedoms
Are not walks over
Here only heads are walked over...

Outlawish

OUTLAWS' LOVE

You called me
Then you shouted at me
That you will kill me.
I took out the gun from the waist
You've stuck the sword in the eye
While my hands
Covered your breasts
The house shook.
You called me
You betrayed me
Why
Beautiful

Baby
What a wretch...

TOYS

I throw pebbles
In the minefield
And...
With eyes closed I look for
The olive piece in you
I get tired when I do not find it.
When I find it I vomit sweetly
The tremor covers me
You'd better run from me
Aicuna
That if we went to sleep
Bastards would get born...

FIGHT

Aicuna was
caught
Giving the thief
Breast milk
That's why they burned her house.
From the window wherefrom
she waved at me
Black smoke came out.
But I wasn't anymore
An outlaw of love
Aiming with the rifle
The target
In the valley
Of raw observation
Among the outlaws
I was look with wonder...

UNEXPLAINED BREAKUP

You do not have me anymore
Nor do I have you
I thought you were brave
Aicuna
What is with this tear in your eye...

COUNTERWATCH

Stay on the plain Aicuna
Propped by the missing
And look crying
Towards the mountain
The minds are tied with scarf
Tonight
You will be attacked
Aicuna
Do not be afraid
That I will become
An exact guerrilla...

INGRATITUDE

Well
Aicuna
You should know that you would be cut
If it weren't for the outlaws...

THE FLOOD

Aicuna has left the herd
Leaving them
The stockings on the wire
He became a hacker
He broke my password
And when he saw
How the heroes betray
Rope or oak
He found nowhere.
Until one day,
unexpectedly
The beauty appeared
On the screen
Advertising condoms
Of the company
"My Love"

Black Parodies

THE MAIN HERO

The hero had been surrounded
From all parts
And he hid in the manor
With a prostitute
Having sex
Deeply despaired
Of the history
That was never
Sung
By lute or ciftelia * ...

* *Albanian folk instrument*

DESPAIR

The unfortunate virgin
Cut her hair
And now angry
Goes to the spring
Never before have her eyes dried up
Since a friend told her:
Aga Hasan became Gay
has a lover in UNMIK...

THE WARRIOR AND THE WOMEN

The warrior went wild in battles
When the woman warrior
Had her menstruation
It was said that very badly
Had the barrel of a gun
Incited her.

ALTAR

To Havzi Nela

A Court with jurisdiction
As Guilty condemned him
To death by hanging in rope
Then ripping off the painter's skin
Who had the courage to draw
A large man sitting
In the horse's instrument.
Gay groups reacted
Pedophils necrophils zoophils
Parties out -
From war from peace.
The Parliament
Europe
Uganda
Kosovo
Writers' Union
Artists journalists
But the Court has not withdrawn
The punishment with the rope
Neither the painter
From the altar...

CURSE

Let this country
Be eaten by dogs
That while still living
Delved us into the ground ...

WATER

Oh, let everything disappear
No snoring
For the time of death
To be found.
No drop
For spraying
The hell fire
Who will
Damp it.

THE MINISTER'S DOG

He walks with it
Through the fair
Every evening.
Both greet the people
When the minister moves his head
It plays with its tail
It barks when he frowns
So well do they understand
Doggish and humanly
At the same time...

With my self

WHEN BARDHI WENT CRAZY

When Bardhi went crazy
People did not run away from him
He ran away from them
He was swearing states and powers
He seemed that
A cock was singing
In the middle of the night.
Watch us Lord
From the eval cock that lies.
He was telling the people
disappear
Raven smell comes your way.
When Bardhi slipped
I went to see him
If he went crazy
For real...

WITH MY SELF

It's hard
But force is needed
Damn you
The Sun has come closer
So hard that
The flame burns you
Damn you
Those who are not are not coming anymore.
Those who are are not enough
You are not sure
If He is with you
And people went up your neck
Along with the power.

It's hard
but we must
Eh
Damn you.

THE OAK

To get up and kill
The best Albanian
It's a curse.
You are not oak
To go back
And kill
The worst.
And a curse is born again.
Is not an oak
The one whose mother cries.
That mother
Is an ax's tail.

THE PUBLIC

Those who dwelt
In the first row,
Often seek their mother.
They never understand art.
The other side is right...
Shines like gold.

THE NORM

Who kills an
Enemy in the battle,
has the right
to kill
ten Albanians
at peacetime...

is this peace?
Gracious heavens of our heads!

THE PATRIOTS

I love more
The country,
He kisses its land then,
He curses himself on stones and slabs.

Do not ask me
because I snap... *

_____
* In the sense that I die ...

THE BIG CLAIM

The hope is
That we will put
The sadness
Alive
In the coffin
And to the traveler
From our hand
We will take
The bundle
Crammed with pain...

EPITAPH

No more verses
Are written
That feelings to the muses
Brought them freedom.
Fuck*
Their mother
How come has the poetry
Died...

---

* *In Albanian, fuck means to put*

CONTENTS

SHORT BIO-BIBLIOGRAPHY / 5
FOREWORD / 7

Dream Exhibition

SUNDAYS DO NOT CALL ME / 13
TEUTA / 14
I REMEMBER YOUR FACE / 15
RESIGNATION / 16
PATHETIC DECLARATION / 17
THE MOON / 18
YOU SLEPT UNDER THE MOON / 19
ANCIENT CITY / 20
HERMETIC / 21
WILL RAIN TOMORROW / 22
YOU BROUGHT THE TIMES
TO SLEEP UNDER THE MOON / 23
TOMORROW / 24
GOOD RAINY NIGHT / 25
IN OUR ABSENCE / 26
THE POETS / 27
WHEN I WILL DIE / 28
DREAMS EXPLANATORY THEORY / 29
PATHS / 30
COMPLEX / 31
CHILLS / 32

Terrible Songs

DEATH PREDICTS / 35
TERRIBLE SONGS / 36
THE POWERFUL / 37
THE FIGHTERS / 39
WAR ATMOSPHERE / 40
POPPY THIEVES / 41
BAPTISMS / 42
REASON / 43
WE / 44
REPORT OF THE HOLY FIGHT / 45
FREE TERRITORIES / 46
THREE DAYS ALBANIA / 47
REPORT OF KOSOVA '99 / 48

Outlawish

OUTLAWS' LOVE / 51
TOYS / 52
FIGHT / 53
UNEXPLAINED BREAKUP / 54
COUNTERWATCH / 55
INGRATITUDE / 56
THE FLOOD / 57

Black Parodies

THE MAIN HERO / 61
DESPAIR / 62
THE WARRIOR AND THE WOMEN / 63
ALTAR / 64

CURSE / 65
WATER / 66
THE MINISTER'S DOG / 67

With my self

WHEN BARDHI WENT CRAZY / 71
WITH MY SELF / 72
THE OAK / 73
THE PUBLIC / 74
THE NORM / 75
THE PATRIOTS / 76
THE BIG CLAIM / 77
EPITAPH / 78

www.ingramcontent.com/pod-product-compliance
Lightning Source LLC
LaVergne TN
LVHW021544080426
835509LV00019B/2820